I0560904

Attack!
of the Killer Man from the Sun!
(Flash Cut)

A Sci-Fi B-Movie Comedy

Presented in TechnicallyColor and 4-Dimensions
(when/where available)

Written by David Andrew Laws

Uproar Theatrics

LICENSING & PRODUCTION INQUIRIES
Uproar Theatrics, LLC.
hello@uproartheatrics.com | www.UproarTheatrics.com

Attack! of the Killer Man from the Sun! copyright © 2023
by David Andrew Laws

Attack! of the Killer Man from the Sun! is published by
Uproar Theatrics, LLC
500 8th Ave FRNT 3, #1714 New York, NY 10018

ISBN: 978-1-968051-26-6

First Printing, May 2025

<u>Cast: (in order)</u>

LOU ION — just an ordinary, everyday scientist
ANNE ION — Lou's ordinary, everyday wife and best friend
SUSAN SMITHS — Lou's favorite-and-only-sister-in-law
SCIENTIST #1 — a man of science
SCIENTIST #2 — a woman of science
SCIENTIST NUMBER THREE — a person of science as
RANGE PARKER — the Park Ranger
ALIEN 1 — an alien from Outside Space
ALIEN 2 — also an alien from the same general vicinity
THE KILLER MAN FROM THE SUN — a killer man from
the Sun
THE ANNOUNCER — himself
and
THE CREATURE — What?? Where??

NOTE: Feel free to double up roles as necessary to suit the
cast size. Suggested doubling for this cut is:

Lou
Anne
Susan
Range Parker/The Killer Man from the Sun
Scientist #1
Scientist #2/The Creature
Scientist #3
The Announcer
Alien 1
Alien 2

NOTE: The stage crew are also indelible parts of this experience,
both backstage and/or in the booth. Don't be afraid to let them be
seen, heard, and otherwise recognized during the action. It is a
play, after all, with every goofy, charming imperfection that that

entails. Don't go overboard with it, and keep them in their traditional black garb if you're going to, but it could be fun.

ANOTHER NOTE: While casting can reflect the pronouns as written, it is equally as appropriate for anyone to play any role. The Killer Man from the Sun can as fittingly be portrayed by a man as by a teenage girl or by a precocious non-binary child or by an extraordinarily-talented peach cobbler. Casting should best reflect the talents available and should be in service of the story being told.

FINAL NOTE, I PROMISE: This show is relentless. The pacing, the humor, the timing; everything in this show is finely attuned to a specific comedy science. In general, the adage is "Louder, Faster, Funnier". But beyond that, this show draws from a variety of sources, and emulating those predecessors can be significantly helpful to capturing the tone, so feel free to study. Not only the black & white B-movies on which it's based, but other media that pokes fun at the genre or are just masters of their own comedic stylings: *Mystery Science Theatre 3000,* Larry Blamire's *The Lost Skeleton of Cadavra,* anything starring Leslie Nielsen, anything written by Douglas Adams. Take things as seriously as you can when they're serious, as silly-ly as you can when you're silly, and have fun with it.

Or don't, what am I gonna do, I'm just an author's note.

I LIED. A FOURTH NOTE: The Aliens do not mispronounce the word "Human" or "Humans". It's not as funny as you think it is. Okay, I'll shut up now. Have fun!

SCENE ONE.

The Ions' Kitchen. Appropriately quaint, as 1950s kitchens were wont to be. There is a kitchen table CS, around which are seated [SL to SR] SCIENTIST #1, LOU, SCIENTIST #2, and SCIENTIST NUMBER THREE. Upstage of them is a blackboard covered in various scientific-looking squiggles. The sounds of birds chirping lightly. Perhaps Rossini's "Call to the Cows".

Additionally, during the following scene [and most others] SCIENTIST NUMBER THREE is completely mute, but still reacts appropriately [albeit silently] to the scenes as they unfold.

ANNOUNCER. *(with gravity)* Attack! Of the Killer Man from the Sun! A Sci-Fi B-Movie Drama for the Stage. Our story begins in the kitchen of the Ion family on a normal, sunny morning. It would normally begin with a prologue introducing, among other things, myself, but this was cut for time. Instead, Lou Ion and the Other Scientists are seated around the kitchen table engaged in a deep and complex scientific discussion.

LOU. Damn! *{note: can be "Darn" or "Dang" or "Heck" or whatever as long as it is a relatively un-scientific interjection}*

SCIENTIST #2. You're right, Lou. We've still got no idea what's causing these massive solar flares. At this rate, the Earth is probably doomed!

SCIENTIST #1. It's not space debris. Not aerosol gases. There must be some part of humanity left to blame.

1

LOU. I just don't understand it. Here we are, the greatest scientific minds of our time, adrift in a sea of answerlessness. If we don't determine the cause of, and thereby the solution to, these solar flares soon, the Earth might be doomed faster than you could say "Oh no, we're being killed by solar flares from our very own Sun! The Earth is doomed and it's too late to do anything about it"!

SCIENTIST #1. *(dropping character slightly)* Is that something people are likely to say?

LOU. They will be if we don't save them, the doomed fools!

ANNOUNCER. Anne Ion, Lou's wife, enters from the kitchen with an ice-cold pitcher of Mrs. Field smith's Brand Lemonade. *(as an ad)* That's Mrs. Fieldsmith's Brand Lemonade. Now with sixty percent more lemonade. But the same amount…of love. *(as the disclaimer at the end of an ad)* Mrs. Fieldsmith's Brand Lemonade contains less than one percent love.

(As he is saying all this, ANNE Ion enters carrying a pitcher of lemonade.)

ANNE. Is that science I hear? Or saving the world?

SCIENTIST #1. Hopefully both, Mrs. Ion.

ANNE. Oh, you. You can just call me Anne.

ANNOUNCER. She winks at the audience.

(She does so. The ANNOUNCER feels the need to explain.)

ANNOUNCER. The joke here is that an 'anion', a-n-i-o-n, is the scientific term for an atom or molecule with a negative charge. The comedy goes perhaps deeper still in that Anne is a character with a constantly positive disposition. But as the first layer of humor will no doubt hardly have landed, there's really no point in delving any deeper.

(If, at this point, the audience laughs, [or, indeed, remains in the theatre] we're golden. Anyway, LOU mimes raising a glass.)

LOU. I'd call you anything you like, dear, for another glass of that lemonade.

(The SCIENTISTS mime raising glasses.)

SCIENTIST #1 & SCIENTIST #2. Mm-hm!

(The chracters all stop and look at their miming with much confusion.)

ANNOUNCER. *(eventually noticing)* Oh! Oh. Oh, sorry, did I not mention that they all have—...? *(flipping back a bit in The Script)* Sorry. It's...not in my—... Anyway. Um. Sorry. In my stage directions earlier, when I was setting the scene, I should have said 'There are glasses on the table'.

(LOU and the other SCIENTISTS each very suddenly place a pair of glasses on the table, either from their own face, a pocket, or the ether. More confusion.)

ANNOUNCER. *(with a sigh)* Drinking glasses.

(LOU and the other SCIENTISTS each produce a drinking glass. They are now very pleased.)

3

ANNOUNCER. And the action continues.

SCIENTIST #1 & SCIENTIST #2. Mm-hm!

ANNE. *(filling the drinking glasses)* I just hope ensuring the fate of mankind doesn't require empty bladders.

LOU. *(taking a drink)* Mmm. *(to the glass of lemonade)* Thanks, sugar. *(to ANNE)* And you too, Anne. Now, if you'll excuse us, we've got a world to save: our own.

ANNE. That's my favorite one!

(They all laugh.)

ANNOUNCER. Offstage, a timer dings.

(There is a dull clunk offstage instead of a ding. The ANNOUNCER looks offstage, annoyed.)

ANNE. Dinner's ready! And my sister will be here any minute. I'll need the table. Lou, honey, say goodbye to your little science pals. The fate of humanity and all of Earth's inhabitants will have to wait.

ANNOUNCER. Anne exits to the kitchen. The Scientists clear the table and exit.

(It is so. If there is a door USL, this is from whence the other SCIENTISTS exit and what LOU closes behind them. If not, they just exit into the void, but not having a door might cause some confusion in some upcoming gags. Either way, LOU returns to the table and sits, doing nothing.)

ANNOUNCER. After an amount of time, the doorbell rings.

(The doorbell buzzes, actually. The ANNOUNCER narrows his eyes, frustrated.)

ANNOUNCER. *(correcting himself through gritted teeth)* …buzzes…

(LOU crosses to the door and opens it. SUSAN enters.)

ANNOUNCER. Lou opens the door and is greeted by Susan, his favorite and oftentimes forgetful sister-in-law.

LOU. Susan! My favorite and oftentimes-forgetful sister-in-law!

SUSAN. Aw, shucks. You're just sayin' that.

ANNOUNCER. Anne re-enters with dinner on a tray.

(Would you believe it? She does just that.)

ANNE. Susan! My favorite and oftentimes-forgetful sister!

SUSAN. Well, gee, aren't I just the bell of the ball tonight? Ding ding.

LOU. Ha ha ha. You certainly are. And oftentimes forgetful.

SUSAN. *(briefly panicked)* Who said that? *(coming back to her senses)* Oh! Hi, Lou!

ANNE. So! Who wants dinner?

LOU. I'm not even sure if I could eat right now, Anne. What with the fate of the world's fate resting in the fate of my hands.

SUSAN. The what of the world's what?

ANNE. Oh, Lou! That was supposed to be a super-top-secret-scientist secret between you and the other top super-top-secret scientists!

LOU. I'm afraid I think she's right, Susan. Susan, I'm afraid I think I'm going to have to ask you to try and forget, or at least not fully comprehend, everything you just heard.

SUSAN. *(cheerily)* That shouldn't be too difficult for me!

(They all laugh, then stop together abruptly.)

LOU. But I think I'm afraid this is no laughing matter we're laughing about. I suppose, since you're family, I could tell you everything. Come, sit at the table with me and, since you're family, I suppose I could tell you everything.

(As they cross to the table, the lights begin to fade to black.)

ANNOUNCER. Lou, Anne, and the oftentimes-forgetful Susan gather around the dinner table, where Lou reveals to her the dangers imminent to the Earth our home. Who knows what horrors he will reveal to her here? We can only speculate, only dream, only imagine the magnitude of the news he must impart unto this most innocent of bystanders.

(As he speaks, the lights rise on the next scene.)

LOU. Well, Susan. Where to begin?—…

ANNOUNCER. Oh! Wait, wait, wait. Is that—… Is that the next scene? That doesn't—…hold on. Shouldn't we—…? *(To whom he is speaking in the above segment [as well as who would theoretically be responding] is unclear.)* Okay, okay. Have it your way. Scene two: still in the kitchen of Lou Ion's home.

SCENE TWO.

Same as Scene One. From SL to SR, the actors are seated ANNE, LOU, SUSAN. The ANNOUNCER is ever-present. If possible, in the transition, SUSAN has had a less-than-subtle costume change.

LOU. Well, Susan. Where to begin?

SUSAN. *(shrugging)* I dunno.

LOU. Well, first off, the world as we know it may be about to become to an end.

SUSAN. Holy mackerel!

LOU. *(with sudden intensity)* What do you know about the mackerel?! *(calming himself)* No, sorry. What I'm referring to is the Sun. You've heard of it?

(SUSAN nods.)

LOU. Good. Well, an increasing number of solar flares have been appearing over the Earth, and they may be quite dangerous. At the rate they're growing, a superflare may soon come into contact with the Earth's atmosphere and ignite the very planet!

SUSAN. Holy cow!

LOU. No, that was my initial suspicion too, but the cows check out. They aren't capable of any kind of organized deification anyway. We've been informed by the government that we, the scientists, are to deal with this problem because, after all, it is science, and that apparently makes it "our problem". I'm afraid I think they're afraid that all this unusual Sun activity may lead to the end of all life on Earth.

SUSAN. Great Scott!

LOU. *(gravely)* No, Scott died trying to solve this dilemma two weeks ago. He died a hero. Now please stop interrupting. We've been monitoring the Sun's rays for some time now.

ANNOUNCER. Lou moves to the blackboard upstage and turns it over, revealing a highly-scientific diagram of the Sun.

(LOU does so, except the picture of the Sun is a big, smiling, yellow cartoon sun with Sunglasses. The ANNOUNCER puts his head in his hand.)

LOU. We've found that it's been producing massive amounts of heat and light for some time now, possibly longer than any of us have been alive, but no one at the government seems too concerned. Still, the activity is definitely possibly deadly, and something must be done. Probably. And that's why I invented…this!

ANNOUNCER. Lou reaches under the table and reveals a marvel of scientific knowledge and ingenuity.

(LOU reaches under the table and picks up the Mysterious Device. It is very low-budget. The ANNOUNCER puts his head in his hands.)

ANNE. Lou, what is that? When did you invent this contraption?

LOU. That's what I do, Anne. I may be a simple Scientist, but deep-down I'm still an inventor at heart. An inventor of things like science, and this.

ANNE. Well, when you put it that way.

SUSAN. But what is it? Did you already tell us and I forgot?

LOU. It's a device that detects that which is dangerous for the planet Earth. But it's been pretty quiet so far.

(He turns a knob on The Device and it begins to blink and beep.)

ANNE. But how will we know if it's working, Lou?

LOU. Oh, when the time comes to know, I think we'll do just that. If my calculatings are correct, whenever something is about to do badness to the Earth, it should make a noise like someone knocking on our front door.

ANNOUNCER. There is a knock on the front door.

(There is.)

ANNE. Like that?

LOU. Exactly like that.

SUSAN. *(panicking)* Should we be panicking??

LOU. No, Susan, I don't think that was The Device. I think that was an actual knock on the actual front door.

ANNE. Oh! I'll get it!

ANNOUNCER. Anne answers the door and is greeted by a park ranger who is looking spiffy.

RANGE PARKER. *(in response to The ANNOUNCER)* Why, thank you.

ANNE. Pardon?

RANGE PARKER. Never mind. Good evening, miss. I hope I'm not troubling you none. Mind if I step inside?

ANNE. No, not at all.

(RANGE PARKER takes one step inside.)

RANGE PARKER. Good evening, folks. I hope I'm not troubling you none. Mind if I take another step inside?

ANNE. Feel free to take as many steps as would make you comfortable, stranger with a hat.

RANGE PARKER. *(taking another step inside and touching the brim of his hat)* Why, thank you. And I do have a hat.

LOU. Good evening, friend. My name is Lou Ion. I'm a scientist. And this is my pleasant wife, Anne Ion.

(ANNE winks at the audience again. A voice offstage [or planted in the audience] says 'Oh, I get it this time!')

LOU. And this is her oftentimes-forgetful sister, Susan.

SUSAN. *(excited)* Hey, that's me!

RANGE PARKER. Good evening, folks. I'm Range Parker. I'm the Park Ranger in this range of the Park.

ANNE. You seem like a very new character. Have we seen you somewhere before?

RANGE PARKER. Nah, my previous scene was cut for time. I was just in the neighborhood of these woods, warning people about the danger out in the woods here.

ANNE. Oh?

LOU. What kind of danger, Ranger Range Parker?

RANGE PARKER. Well, I'm on the lookout for a creature.

SUSAN. A creature??

RANGE PARKER. What?? Where??

SUSAN. No, sorry. I just meant… *(so as not to alarm him)* …a Creature?

RANGE PARKER. Ahem. Yes, well. You folks haven't seen anything suspicious in the park, have you?

LOU. Suspicious? Like how?

RANGE PARKER. Oh, I don't know. Suspicious like a ravenous, blood-thirsty beast rampaging through the countryside is how!

LOU. *(frightened)* Well, when you put it that way! *(realizing; back to normal)* No, we haven't seen anything like that, have we, dear?

ANNE. No, not that I remember. And I think I'd remember something like that.

SUSAN. I might not.

(RANGE PARKER looks at her suspiciously. After a moment, LOU realizes and starts to laugh, which starts everyone to laughing. They stop together on LOU's line.)

LOU. Ranger Parker, are you trying to tell us something?

RANGE PARKER. *(pulling out and unfolding a piece of paper)* Well, I don't know how to say this, folks, but… there's been a…there's been a…

LOU. A what, Parker? Spit it out!

RANGE PARKER. I told you I don't know how to say it!

LOU. Oh! …oh. I'm sorry. Let me see. *(Takes the note. Reading it aloud:)* "There's been a homicide in the forest." Oh. *(realizing)* There's been a homicide in the forest??

SUSAN. What's that??

LOU. What?! Where?!

SUSAN. No, what's a homicide?

RANGE PARKER. Oh, that's easy! It means there's been a murder in the place where all the trees like to be close together. I came down here to warn you folks to stay inside with your doors locked and your windows barred.

LOU. Ranger Parker, doesn't that seem a little extreme?

RANGE PARKER. Well, I wouldn't know about all that, Mr. Ion. But this was no ordinary murder. The bodies of the victims were found...charred to the bone. It was as if they'd been engulfed by a flame. Like a fire. Or. The Sun?

(LOU and ANNE gasp. SUSAN gasps too, a moment too late.)

ANNE. Lou, you don't think—

LOU. On the contrary, Anne. I think quite a lot, and sometimes for long periods at a time. And what I'm thinking in this moment is that maybe this 'homicide', if we wish to call it that, may have something to do with the possibly deadly solar flares being not so "possibly deadly" after all!

ANNOUNCER. Interruptingly, there is another knock at the door!

(You know what? There is.)

LOU. Hmm. That still wasn't The Device. That was another actual knock at the front door.

RANGE PARKER. *(a bit too excited)* Maybe it's the creature!

ANNE. What?? Where??

LOU. No, no. See, I have a Device here that makes a knocking sound whenever it detects danger.

RANGE PARKER. *(disappointed that it's not something dangerous)* Oh…

ANNE. Who could that be at this hour?

SUSAN. Maybe it's me.

ANNE. Hush, dear.

ANNOUNCER. Anne moves to open the door.

(ANNE goes to the door and opens it.)

ANNOUNCER. She is greeted by two figures whose scenes were also cut for time. And what she can never know, but is of the utmost importance to understanding basically everything that these characters get up to is that this is a pair of aliens from outside space! Their ship crashed in the forest while they were on the hunt for the creature that has been plaguing the forest with its murdersome ways. They have disguised themselves as humans and found their way to the humble Ion home in search of companions to face this deadly foe.

LOU. Who is it, honey?

ANNE. Well, I don't know, but we've been standing here for a long time now.

(LOU joins her at the door.)

LOU. Hello. Won't you come in?

ALIEN 1. Hello. I don't know. Won't we?

(There is an awkward pause.)

RANGE PARKER. Is it the deadly forest creature?

(This pulls the ALIENS into the room.)

ALIEN 2. You are seeking The Creature as well?

RANGE PARKER. I mean, I don't like to brag, but warning all you fine folks about the deadly animals in these parts of the park is exactly what makes me the best park ranger to have ever existed. Ever.

LOU. *(to the ALIENS)* My name is Lou Ion. I'm a scientist. And this is my pleasant wife, Anne Ion.

(This time, the offstage voice or audience plant laughs uproariously at the joke. It is abrupt.)

LOU. This is my favorite, but oftentimes-forgetful sister-in-law Susan. And this is our new acquaintance Park Ranger Range Parker.

(Slight pause as they all wait for a response.)

ANNE. *(to the ALIENS)* And you are?

(There is another pause until the ALIENS realize that the others are awaiting a response.)

ALIEN 1. Yes, we are.

LOU. *(a little more leadingly)* Yes, but you are…

ALIEN 2. We do not require hydration. Thank you.

ANNE. No, no. What are your names?

(A look of panic crosses the ALIENS' faces. They look at each other, then back at the others.)

ALIEN 1. Excuse us for one Earth moment I mean moment.

(The others nod. The ALIENS gather DSR. As they talk, the others continue looking at them or back and forth from one another, but are totally aware that their new guests are having an aside.)

ALIEN 2. What is a name??? What, by the visual magnitude of transneptunian conjunction is a name???

ANNOUNCER. The first of the aliens reveals a device that looks exactly like the one invented by Lou Ion, that is to say, a technological marvel far beyond our human comprehension.

(The ALIENS do have a Device. It is just like LOU's, that is to say, bad.)

ALIEN 1. Not to fear, my elliptical orbit. We shall consult The Device. Besides its primary function of disguising us as humans and its secondary function of tracking The Creature, it has a tertiary function that can define any archaic terminology these humans may be using.

(ALIEN 1 consults The Device. Maybe it dings. Either way, he has the information he needs.)

ALIEN 1. Aha! Well it's very quite simple really. A "name" is a set of nomenclature by which a person, animal, place, or thing is known, addressed, or referred to. We must assign ourselves Earth nomenclature so that the humans do not think us to be odd or strange or great gibbering sacks of nameless flesh.

ALIEN 2. You speak truth, my cosmonaut of desire. But what human name shall we both use?

ALIEN 1. More than that, we will need to come up with multiple names! One for each of us, at least.

ALIEN 2. But what even does a human name sound like? Is Blorf a human name? Is Applebapper? What about Steve? Oh, this is too much…

(ALIEN 2 begins to faint. ALIEN 1 catches her. The Humans look on worriedly.)

ANNE. Everything alright over there?

ALIEN 1. Everything is fine! Do not begin to suspect anything!

(He helps ALIEN 2 to her feet.)

ALIEN 1. Do not fret, my spectroscope of passion. The Device has a quaternary function as well.

ALIEN 2. *(sarcastically)* Oh, of course it does! Next you will be telling me it has a quinary function! Then a senary, then a septenary!

ALIEN 1. No, no, it can only do four things. Any more than that would be ridiculous. I will set The Device to quickly scan through the entirety of the human vocabulary to isolate for us the most perfectly average and most blending-in names imaginable.

ALIEN 2. Well, quickly, my dearest! Before the humans begin to suspect anything.

LOU. Are you beginning to suspect anything?

ANNE. *(considering)* Mmm. No.

LOU. *(pleased)* Me neither.

(ALIEN 1 adjusts some knobs on The Device and reads from it.)

ALIEN 1. There! Our names shall be foolproof for proving fools of the humans. We have been assigned the most ordinary and commonplace names imaginable.

(The ALIENS turn back to the others, smiling pleasantly. Everyone in the room tries to act like what just happened wasn't weird.)

ALIEN 1. Hello! And thank you for your patience. My name is Pants. And this is my wife— *(checking the readout, then confidently)* Neil Patrick Harris.

(There is an expectant pause.)

ANNE. Ah. Pants. That's an interesting name. What's your last name?

ALIEN 2. *(with ferocious intensity)* That is the last name we shall give you, and we will speak no more of names!

(There is a brief awkward pause.)

ALIEN 1. You must excuse my wife. She is allergic to names.

LOU. Well, it's a pleasure to make your acquaintances. What can we do for you?

ALIEN 1. Oh, it is not what you can do for us, Mr. Ion. But what we can do for each other.

ALIEN 2. Yes, we too are seeking… *(carefully)* The Creature. And have done so for some time now.

ANNE. Lou, do you think this has anything to do with the possibly deadly solar activity?

LOU. More than that, Anne, I think it has everything to do with the possibly deadly solar activity!

SUSAN. *(pointing at ALIEN 1's Device)* Oh! And they have a that!

LOU. By science, you're right, Susan. That's a remarkably similar device to one of my own. *(holding up his Device)* This one, in fact.

ALIEN 1. It's true! You must be a remarkable specimen of human ingenuity.

LOU. Well, that was my nickname in high school.

RANGE PARKER. Welp! I'm just realizing I haven't said anything in a while. I must be done in this scene. Goodnight, everyone.

(RANGE PARKER goes to leave.)

ANNE. But wait! Park Ranger Range Parker! The Creature!

(Everyone does the "What?? Where??" gag, except SUSAN doesn't realize and goes a little late.)

SUSAN. Where, what?? *(mumbling)* Aw, shoot, I didn't do it right…

ANNE. No, I just meant, will you be safe out there in the park? What about The Creature?

RANGE PARKER. *(dramatically, as if it's the last time he'll ever seen any of these nice people)* I don't know, Mrs. Ion. But if this is the last time I ever see any of you nice people, remember me as I was. A park ranger. And a damn *{note: can be "dang" or "darn"}* good one. One who took the necessary risks to protect the people who loved him…and the park he loved…to range. *(suddenly back to upbeat)* Bye now!

(RANGE PARKER exits whistling.)

LOU. *(momentarily reflective)* What an interesting man. *(back to business)* Anyway. This matter of life and death isn't going to stop about itself!

ALIEN 1. If we are understanding you correctly, science man, our purposes are aligned.

LOU. Yes, I think they are.

ALIEN 2. And more than that, we should be working in tandem.

SUSAN. Like a bicycle!

ANNE. Susan, please.

LOU. And more than that, I think we could learn a thing or two from one another.

ANNE. Yes, I believe we could.

ALIEN 1. I believe we will learn more from you than you may realize, but you will also learn more from us about much more than you may realize as well.

SUSAN. I've already forgotten. What was that man with the hat's name?

ANNE. Oh, Susan.

(ANNE & LOU have a laugh at silly SUSAN. The ALIENS, blending in, try to replicate the sound [laughter] as well, with a moderate amount of success.)

ANNOUNCER. There is another knock at the front door!

(The characters onstage turn towards the door expectantly.)

ANNOUNCER. Or…wait. No.

(As he checks his notes, the characters peer at him from their peripheries and over their shoulders, trying to remain in place)

ANNOUNCER. It's…which knock is this? Sorry, there are so many sound cues in this—…okay, hold on, "should be working in tandem, blah blah blah." Ah! Yep, nope. It's—…Okay, sorry. It's not the door. But we don't know that yet. Sorry. So, I'll just say: There is a knock! And that's…that's it.

(There is, not from the door, but from The Device.)

ANNE. Oh! I'll get it!

(ANNE goes to answer the door. There's no one there.)

ANNOUNCER. Anne goes to answer the door. There's no one there.

ANNE. *(gasps)* There's no one there!

(Bum bum BUMMMMMM)

LOU. I don't think it was the door that was knocking, Anne. Or anyone at the door. I think The Device is suddenly performing its purported purpose! I'm almost certain of it!

(Another knock, very clearly from The Device.)

LOU. Now I'm entirely certain of it!

22

(The ALIENS' device makes a sound as well, something more technological and alien.)

LOU. What was that?

ALIEN 1. *(to ALIEN 2)* Should we inform them yet about The Device's multi-faceted functionality?

ALIEN 2. I do not think so yet, my phantom menace.

ALIEN 1. Then I will tell them a lie. *(back to the group)* My stomachs were grumbling because I am very sleepy.

ANNE. Oh, that's right! I'd nearly forgotten about dinner!

SUSAN. *(drippingly facetious)* And I thought forgetting things was my distinguishing characteristic.

LOU. Anne, dinner will have to wait! If we don't follow the signal, there will possibly almost be no time left to lose!

ANNE. Lou Ion, I did not do whatever goes on in a kitchen over a hot stove all afternoon so that you could save the world on an empty stomach.

LOU. Well, when you put it that way. And I'm actually pretty hungry myself. But there'll be no time for dessert!

ANNE. The life of a scientist's wife!

(ANNE exits to the kitchen.)

LOU. Pants, Neil Patrick Harris, will you join us for dinner?

ALIEN 1. Before we take part in your eating ritual, I would like to introduce this. *(pulling a small stone from his pocket)* It is a rare metal called McGuffininium, and it may come in useful should we need to power up any world-saving devices at a later point. Carrying it has become cumbersome due to an excuse I am making up and not the more intense gravity on this planet. Would one of you hold it in case it is needed to face the trials ahead?

LOU. *(taking the stone)* Well, I would, but my hands will probably be too full of science. And Anne's not in the room right now. Susan! Why don't you hold onto this McGuffininium for safekeeping?

SUSAN. *(pocketing the stone)* Okie dokie.

LOU. Let's hope the meal Anne's prepared is especially delicious. Because if we don't finish this and get out there to do some science soon, this might be the last meal anyone ever eats.

(Dramatic music and fade to black. The curtain closes as The ANNOUNCER speaks.)

ANNOUNCER. Now, traditionally, this is where we would take an intermission, but that too was cut for time. In fact, why don't I go ahead and give you a lowdown on everything that was cut for time so that we can stop mentioning it? *(reading from a separate piece of paper)* Range Parker Park Ranger's scene with Teen Guy and Teen Girl and the subsequent deaths of all three of those characters; any scenes or mentions of the military characters Private Browser, Private Public, and Senior Officer Major "Sergeant" Lieutenant Private Jr.; Lou's long-lost fraternal twin brother Ian Ion; two different romantic subplots; a construction montage; and a very elaborately choreographed but tastefully done nude scene between—... You know what, let's just say there was a lot cut for time and move on.

So. With that acting as our intermission, let's all feel very refreshed, pretend our legs are nice and stretched, and move on to–

SCENE THREE.

Deep in the forest. Moonlit trees either well-made or clearly cardboard. If available, a light mist blankets the ground.

As The ANNOUNCER speaks, LOU, ANNE, SUSAN, ALIEN 1, and ALIEN 2 reenter. LOU and ALIEN 1 each have an identical Mysterious Device, and each Device is blinking and beeping softly. SUSAN has had a costume change.

ANNOUNCER. –the thrilling conclusion of Attack! of the Killer Man from the Sun! When we last left our heroes, the scene they were in was cut for time. Shoot! I said I wasn't going to mention that anymore. In any case, we now find them venturing forth into the unknown horrors of the Mourning Wood Forest *{note: can be "Hickeyneck Woods"}.* Devices at the ready, they scour the site for danger, hoping to stumble upon it before it stumbles upon them, when suddenly!

(The characters tense in preparation.)

ANNOUNCER. Both Mysterious Devices stop blinking and beeping.

(Both Mysterious Devices stop blinking and beeping.)

25

LOU. Look! Listen!

ANNE. But I don't see and/or hear anything!

LOU. My point exactly!

ANNE. What was your point exactly?

LOU. That you don't see and/or hear anything. My device only has a limited range of no more than one hundred miles, but not less than one hundred and fifty feet. Which means the danger must be close. I can only assume our companion's device is as similar in doing as it is in looking. And that's why you don't see and/or hear anything!

ANNE. *(pointing offstage)* But I do and/or do! Is that the Creature?

LOU, ANNE, ALIEN 1, ALIEN 2, SUSAN. What?? Where??

(The KILLER MAN FROM THE SUN enters from the direction ANNE was indicating.)

KILLER MAN FROM THE SUN. It is I: me!

ALIEN 1. Okay, good news bad news, that is not the creature.

SUSAN. Great merciful heavens!

ALIEN 2. Very good, Susan! That's exactly where it came from! Right up there in the heavens. The Sun to be precise!

LOU. Of course! He's the product of all these potentially deadly solar flares!

KILLER MAN FROM THE SUN. I am the embodiment of your Sun, puny humans!

ALIEN 2. Who are you calling humans?

ALIEN 1. Us, dear.

ALIEN 2. Oh, yes, that's right. We are those.

KILLER MAN FROM THE SUN. I have been watching over your planet since its creation and have made my final judgement. You are unworthy as a species to continue your pathetic existences.

LOU. Oh. Well. I'm sure we can figure out a way to solve that. Surely there's some sort of compromise to be reached, right?

KILLER MAN FROM THE SUN. No.

LOU. No?

KILLER MAN FROM THE SUN. No.

ANNE. No?

KILLER MAN FROM THE SUN. No.

ALIEN 1. No?

KILLER MAN FROM THE SUN. No.

ALIEN 2. No?

KILLER MAN FROM THE SUN. No.

SUSAN. Are you sure?

KILLER MAN FROM THE SUN. No. I mean, yes. Darn it.

(pause)

LOU. No?

KILLER MAN FROM THE SUN. *(angrily)* No.

LOU. Well…what happens next then?

KILLER MAN FROM THE SUN. I am judge, jury, and executioner. You will all be terminated.

(The characters look amongst themselves with confusion.)

KILLER MAN FROM THE SUN. To death!

(The characters react with fear.)

ANNE. Lou! What can we do?

ALIEN 1. Yes, Lou. It seems you have been elected the impromptu leader of us all, about which I am not bitter in any way. What can we do?

LOU. I'm not sure! If only so much of the story hadn't been cut for time!

(SCIENTIST #2 and SCIENTIST NUMBER THREE enter.)

SCIENTIST #2. Lou!

LOU. Two of the three scientists! But where's Scientist 1?

SCIENTIST #2. He was cut for time. But that's not important! We've brought you a deus ex machina! Here, catch!

(SCIENTIST #2 throws LOU an identical copy of the previous Mysterious Devices. LOU does not catch it because of how bad the throw was)

LOU. That was a very bad throw.

SCIENTIST #2. I'm a scientist, not a baseball doctor!

KILLER MAN FROM THE SUN. I tire of your shenanigrams. I begin charging my beam of death…NOW!

ANNOUNCER. The Killer Man from the Sun begins to charge his deadly beam of death, ensuring the death of all life on Earth.

ANNE. Oh no! What'll we do, Lou?

LOU. Well, if the Scientists have brought us this third device, they must have discovered some information that would make it useful.

SCIENTIST #2. We have! The Sun man is made of energy from the Sun.

LOU. Okay, you've lost me.

SCIENTIST #2. His formation must have had something to do with all of these recent solar flares. If we combine the power of all three devices, we can create the exact opposite conditions of a solar flare—…

LOU. …—and send the Sun man back to where he came from in space! That's brilliant! Why didn't we think of that?

ANNE. But you did!

LOU. Oh yeah. I guess you're right!

(LOU and ALIEN 1 go about constructing a new device using all three Mysterious Devices. The others cheer them on, and the KILLER MAN continues to charge.)

KILLER MAN FROM THE SUN. Any last words, Earth things? My mighty beam of death is at 99% readiness!

ALIEN 1. And ours is at one hundred percent readiness!

(LOU brandishes a totally new Device, which looks a lot like the previous devices taped together.)

LOU. Prepare to be defeated, Sun Man!

ANNOUNCER. Using this totally new device, Lou envelops the Sun Creature in what, for budgetary purposes, can only be described. But it can be described as a beam of powerful energy, which wraps around the Sun man, momentarily stunning him.

ALIEN 1. It's working, Lou.

LOU. Yes! I can feel it! It's working!

KILLER MAN FROM THE SUN. No, it isn't, idiot.

ANNOUNCER. Though the machine is mighty, it is not nearly enough to overcome the power of the sun! With a blast of energy from the Sun Man's hand, the Device falls from Lou's grip, useless and silent.

(Ideally, the New Device falls from LOU's hand with as loud a clattering as possible.)

ANNE. What have we done that's so deplorable, Mister Man from the Sun? What's your problem with us Earth folk anyway?

KILLER MAN FROM THE SUN. Foolish humanity. For eons, I have provided you with life-sustaining heat and light.

LOU. I knew it!

KILLER MAN FROM THE SUN. And how do you repay me? By polluting not only your own planet, but the galaxy around you with useless satellites and mountains of trash. The solar system does not belong to you! It is mine!! Without me you are nothing!!!

SUSAN. Well, someone woke up on the wrong side of the universe this morning.

KILLER MAN FROM THE SUN. I tire of this banter. Prepare for being dead!

ANNOUNCER. The Killer Man from the Sun attacks! Our heroes face their foe in thrilling hand-to-hand combat.

(LOU and The KILLER MAN from the Sun grapple. The other SCIENTISTS join in, but are quickly thrown aside. Then the ALIENS join in, but are equally discarded. The choreography is all...just...just awful...)

ANNOUNCER. But just as it seems that Lou Ion has met his match, he is struck with the memory of vital importance.

LOU. *(as he fights)* Of course! How could I have been so forgetful? If I can supercharge the New Device, it will put an end to this in an instant. But the only way to generate that much power would be—... Of course! How could I have been so forgetful? Quickly, Susan, toss me the Device. And...the McGuffininium!!

SUSAN. Sorry, the what now?

(LOU and the KILLER MAN are still fighting, but it's turned into the same three 'punch and block' moves on a loop.)

LOU. The rare metal given to me by Pants that he said might be useful should we need to power up any world-saving devices at a later point but that had become cumbersome due to an excuse he was making up and not the more intense gravity on this planet, which I couldn't carry because my hands were probably going to be too full of science, and Anne wasn't in the room, so I gave it to you for safekeeping!

SUSAN. Oh! That McGuffininium. I've got it right—... *(checking her pockets or lack thereof)* Oh no! I must've forgotten it in my costume change!

LOU. By the Science gods! Who could have possibly foreseen this outcome?!

ANNOUNCER. What will our heroes do? Without the McGuffininium, how will they prevail? What can save them now? *(suddenly defiant; he's had enough)* You know what? I'm tired of things getting cut for time. I'm writing this one back in.

(The ANNOUNCER uses a pen to scribble in the Script.)

ANNOUNCER. From the depths of the woods comes a tertiary adversary, an unlikely ally against this solar menace. With razor sharp claws and a menacing roar, our party comes face to face at long last with…the Creature!

(Everyone goes What?? Where??, even The KILLER MAN FROM THE SUN.)

ANNOUNCER. That!! There!!

(The ANNOUNCER points offstage where The CREATURE enters. It is a big, ridiculous space beast like the movie monsters of old. The more it looks like a person in a giant suit, the better. Epic music plays as The CREATURE does battle with The KILLER MAN FROM THE SUN. Everyone else steps back and watches in amazement. Finally, The KILLER MAN stumbles, falls, and The CREATURE seems victorious. Everyone cheers. But then, The CREATURE grabs ANNE in his creature-y arms.)

ANNE. Lou!

LOU. Anne!

SUSAN. Why does no one ever cry out <u>my</u> name in panic?

(Everyone tries unsuccessfully to save ANNE from The CREATURE.)

ANNOUNCER. What ill luck! Just when our heroes thought their troubles were over, a new batch of danger has suddenly appeared. What lengths will they go through to defeat this new foe? How many more scenes will be dedicated to the eradication of this deadly beast? What will—…

(The KILLER MAN explodes The CREATURE with a fireball, killing it. The CREATURE falls.)

ANNOUNCER. Well. I tried.

KILLER MAN FROM THE SUN. Foolish mortals! No mere Creature can stop me! Prepare to finally suffer my final wrath! Prepare to witness the full power of the all-consuming Sun!

ALIEN 2. *(to ALIEN 1)* Farewell, my supplemental appendage.

ALIEN 1. I love you, Neil Patrick Harris.

ANNE. Oh, Lou! What's going to happen to us?

LOU. I'm afraid I think…this is the end for us…I'm afraid.

(Everyone freezes and stares at SCIENTIST NUMBER THREE as they [finally] speak.)

SCIENTIST NUMBER THREE. It is for the best! Humanity was doomed of its own accord. Better this swift cleansing action than the inevitable destruction we would have rained down upon ourselves. Look at the world we have created:

divided. Hedonistic. Careening from one biological disaster to the next societal war — we are mess of civilizations still ruled by our primal instincts when the only true scarcities are the ones we impose upon ourselves. Intelligence is mocked and self-importance is embraced. We fear, we mistrust, we lie and are lied to by those that swear themselves our leaders.

Then where will we be led? Only to sorrow. Only to despair. Only to death. I implore this benevolent being to save us from our own self-slaughter. I have seen too many atrocities carried out in the name of science, too many evils committed in the name of humanity. I only ask that our demise at your hands may be swift, painless, and merciful.

ANNOUNCER. A harsh reality rings from every word of Scientist Number Three's speech. Their fate surely sealed, our heroes huddle together to await the verdict of the morally-justified killer man of the Sun.

KILLER MAN FROM THE SUN. My space ears have heard your plea, human. But your request has been…denied. Your life is no longer in my hands. Your desire for change has touched my flaming heart.

LOU. You mean, you've changed your opinion of us?

KILLER MAN FROM THE SUN. No.

ANNE. No?

KILLER MAN FROM THE SUN. No.

SCIENTIST #2. No?

KILLER MAN FROM THE SUN. Stop that. I have not changed my opinion of you. You are a greedy, emotional people who will soon drive themselves to the brink of non-existence without my intervening. Fear is in your very nature and at a constant war with your ability to love. But I see within your kind hope yet. The ability to identify one's mistakes denotes the ability…to change. Perhaps it is not too late for you. I will still be watching, Earth. But with a more optimistic eye.

ANNOUNCER. With a final nod of his head, the entity from the Sun teleports back to the cosmos above.

(They all look on expectantly. The KILLER MAN FROM THE SUN contemplates for a moment, then points dramatically off-right.)

KILLER MAN FROM THE SUN. Look! Another Creature!

(As everyone does the What?? Where?? one final time. The KILLER MAN FROM THE SUN runs off SL. Once he's gone, the others all look around in awe as if he had disappeared.)

ANNOUNCER. As the dust settles, the crew of Earth-saving saviors gather together once more to gaze up in wonder at the wonder they had just maintained: our Sun. Source of all life, a mighty beacon of hope, and…actually really bad to stare at for long periods of time. …guys?

(Everyone stops looking up except poor SUSAN.)

ANNE. Well, you've done it, husband of mine. Saved the Earth, and it's not even bedtime.

LOU. Don't thank me, honey. *(puts his hand on SCIENTIST NUMBER THREE's shoulder)* Well, never mind, you can thank me if you want.

(SCIENTIST NUMBER THREE frowns.)

LOU. But in our own way, we've all made a difference. Without the Scientists, we might never have known about the threat in the first place. Pants, Neil Patrick Harris, your fortuitous arrival helped us locate the strange man from the Sun. That Park Ranger with the odd name warned us about the danger and also had a hat. Anne, without your love and support, I may never even have become a scientist in the first place. And Susan—

(Everyone looks to SUSAN who is still staring up at the Sun.)

LOU. Well…Susan was there too.

ANNE. But how will we obey the commands set by the man from the Sun? He's expecting change, and if there's one thing humanity is fairly averse to doing, it's to be doing just that.

LOU. There's much truth in what you say. But when our backs are against the wall, or the Sun, in this case, we always find a way to survive. And I'm sure if we band together, we can improve ourselves and make our Sun proud.

SUSAN. *(re-joining the group)* And I was there too!

(Everyone laughs.)

LOU. Wait a minute! I've got it! The answer to it all! It's been staring us in the face the whole time; I can't believe I didn't see it before! A way to appease our Sun and maintain our fickle humanity. It's so simple! All we have to—

(Blackout. Projection reading "Scene Cut For Time". If a projection is not available, The ANNOUNCER says "I'm so sorry, the end of that scene seems to have been also cut for time" before a blackout.)

EPILOGUE.

Lights up on just the ANNOUNCER. The rest of the cast has been cleared or have their focus on him.

ANNOUNCER. A few months later, Lou received the coveted Science Award for his efforts in protecting the Earth that fateful day. Anne also received three-fourths of a Science Award, but was more gratified that her Apple Crumble Pie won the blue ribbon at the State Fair. Susan, in a series of events completely unrelated to the happenings of this story, became a best-selling author of the self-help classic "Looking for Gloves in All the Wrong Places". Scientists One and Two donated The Creature's body to a museum and then ran away together to Iceland, where they currently live as underwater circus performers. Pants and Neil Patrick Harris are currently raising two beautiful children in a gorgeous Harlem Townhouse in New York City. Range Parker the Park Ranger's portion of the epilogue was cut for time.

As for me? I kept on telling this story, because it must be told. The Sun watches over us all, and attention must be paid. I don't know if we'll ever get a visit like that again, but if we do, I hope humanity is just a little bit more prepared. The End. *(mysteriously)* Or is it? *(checks the script, then cheerfully)* Op! Yep. It is. The End. Goodnight!

END

www.ingramcontent.com/pod-product-compliance
Lightning Source LLC
Chambersburg PA
CBHW031239120626
46545CB00003B/1198